Letting Go

BY THE SAME AUTHORS
JULIA C. DAVIS

Empowering English Language Learners (contributing author)

Specialist Fourth Class John Joseph DeFazio: Advocating For Disabled American Veterans (contributing author)

An Artistic Tribute to Harriet Tubman (coeditor)

The Commission (contributing author)

Finding a Better Way (contributing author)

The Christian World Liberation Front (contributing author)

Jesus among the Homeless (contributing author)

Otto & The White Dove (contributing author)

JEANNE C. DEFAZIO

Creative Ways to Build Christian Community (edited with John P. Lathrop)

How to Have an Attitude of Gratitude on the Night Shift (coauthor with Teresa Flowers)

Redeeming the Screens (edited with William David Spencer)

Berkeley Street Theatre: How Improvisation and Street Theater Emerged as Christian Outreach to the Culture of the Time (editor)

Empowering English Language Learners (edited with William David Spencer)

Keeping the Dream Alive: A Reflection on the Art of Harriet Lorence Nesbitt (author and editor)

Specialist Fourth Class John Joseph DeFazio: Advocating for Disabled American Veterans (editor)

Christian Egalitarian Leadership (contributing author).

An Artistic Tribute to Harriet Tubman (coeditor).

The Commission (editor).

Finding a Better Way (editor)
The Christian World Liberation Front (author)
Jesus among the Homeless (contributing author)
Otto & The White Dove (editor)

TERRY MCDERMOTT

Trail of Tears (author)
Otto & The White Dove (contributing author)
Poetry
"The Crimson Wall"
"The Day before Tomorrow"
"A Child's Lament"
"Never Said Goodbye"
"A Smile Sadder than Tears"
"The Fifth Vote"
"Grace Alone"
"A Prayer for All Mothers"
"Color Me Dead"
"Death Roe"
"The American Lie"
"Blood on a Shoe"
"I Am an American"
"A Song Never Sung"
"Through the Eyes of Jesus"
"Double Cross"
"Many Tears Ago"
"If Only I Had Known"

Letting Go

JEANNE C. DEFAZIO
& TERRY MCDERMOTT
Foreword by Julia C. Davis

RESOURCE *Publications* · Eugene, Oregon

LETTING GO

Copyright © 2024 Jeanne C. DeFazio and Terry McDermott. All rights reserved. Except for brief quotations in critical publications or reviews, no part of this book may be reproduced in any manner without prior written permission from the publisher. Write: Permissions, Wipf and Stock Publishers, 199 W. 8th Ave., Suite 3, Eugene, OR 97401.

Resource Publications
An Imprint of Wipf and Stock Publishers
199 W. 8th Ave., Suite 3
Eugene, OR 97401

www.wipfandstock.com

PAPERBACK ISBN: 979-8-3852-1265-1
HARDCOVER ISBN: 979-8-3852-1266-8
EBOOK ISBN: 979-8-3852-1267-5

02/05/24

Scripture quotations marked NIV are taken from the Holy Bible, New International Version,*NIV.* Copyright © 1973, 1978, 1984, 2011 by Biblica, Inc. Used by permission of Zondervan. All rights reserved. www.zondervan.com.

Scripture quotations marked NASB are taken from the New American Standard Bible*, Copyright © 1960, 1962, 1963, 1968, 1971, 1972, 1973, 1975, 1977, 1995 by The Lockman Foundation. Used with permission.

Letting go of fear, regret, and anger, I thank God for covering my past, present, and future.

JEANNE DEFAZIO

Contents

Foreword by Julia C. Davis | xi

Acknowledgements | xiii

CHAPTER 1

    White Ribbon Day | 3

    A Prayer for All Mothers | 5

    Grace Alone | 6

    Lonely Arms | 7

    A Dad and His Daughter | 9

    Lonely Teardrops | 10

    The Day before Tomorrow | 12

    Forever Winter | 13

    Storm the Heavens | 14

    Beyond Baby Blue | 15

    When Jesus Walked | 16

    My Heart's Cry | 18

    A Mother's Lament | 19

    Silent Suffering | 20

Handle with Prayer | 21

What Happened to Your Blood? | 22

The Storyteller | 24

Runaway | 25

Tears | 26

A White Boy's Blues | 27

Martin Luther King Hall | 29

CONCLUSION | 32

About the Authors | 33

Bibliography | 37

Foreword

JULIA C. DAVIS

As AN EDUCATOR, I used art to help at-risk, multicultural students heal. Research identifies art as a conduit to individual and collective well-being:

> Access to arts opportunities and participation in the arts can dramatically improve health outcomes and well-being, counter inequalities and increase social engagement. As a supplement to medicine and care, the evidence suggests that engagement with the arts can improve a person's physical and mental well-being. The benefits of arts activities are being seen beyond traditional settings, and their role in supporting communities and individuals who would otherwise be excluded is increasingly being recognised.[1]

As an African American woman, I am concerned about these statistics:

> Among the 33 areas that reported race by ethnicity data for 2021, non-Hispanic White (White) women and non-Hispanic Black (Black) women accounted for the highest percentages of all abortions (30.2% and 41.5%, respectively), and Hispanic women and non-Hispanic women in the other race category accounted for lower percentages (21.8% and 6.5%, respectively) (Table 6).[2]

---

1. Welsh NHS Confederation, "Arts, Health and Well-Being," 1.
2. Kortsmit et al., "Abortion Surveillance," 6.

Foreword

I am participating in this project because I love the fact that Terry McDermott is publishing his poetry to comfort women suffering from postabortion depression.

> One of the greatest works of mercy is the gift of comfort. To accompany our brothers and sisters in all moments, but especially in the most difficult ones, is to practice the behavior of Jesus. He sympathized with the pain of others and offered the joy of the gospel.[3]

Letting go is one of the most powerful lessons I have learned in life. Art appreciation has been a creative strategy of mine to let go. I often sing traditional African American "spirituals" to let go of past hurts, pains and fears. Stuck in traffic in the tunnel, I belt out old Negro Spirituals that give me strength and keep my spirits up and prevent road rage. As a Christian, I find love, acceptance, and freedom by letting go. I love this book because it reminds us all that God forgives, loves, and wraps his everlasting arms of love around us as we let go of any fear, regret, or anger and thank him for covering our past, present and future.

Moses was guided by God who instructed him to march his people out of Egypt. Moses told the people not to be afraid, to "stand still, and see the salvation of the Lord" (Exod 14:13, KJV). And they did. I say this "letting go" prayer daily to express my surrender, faith, and hope in God: "I will stand still and see the salvation of my God." Letting go of my past and trusting God with my life each day brings me peace and happiness.

---

3. Mathis, *Jesus among the Homeless*, 74.

Acknowledgements

THANKING ALL THE GREAT visual and performing artists who inspired me to let go of my past and empowered me to take hold of my future. I am grateful for national arts leaders who made art freely available. Special thanks to Governor Jerry Brown for creating the California Council of Arts and to Senator Jay Rockefeller for his active support of education, healthcare, and the arts. Congratulations to Father Mauro Mantovani! Pope Francis has appointed him prefect of the Vatican Library. Thanks to Caleb Loring III and Peter Lynch for their support and kindness. Grateful to my brother in Christ Ed Moore who always makes me laugh. I thank Jesus for giving me the strength to carry on.

JEANNE DEFAZIO

Chapter 1

Letting Go and Letting God

JEANNE DEFAZIO AND TERRY MCDERMOTT

JEANNE DEFAZIO:
THE ARTS ARE KEY to the ability to let go of hurts, pains, anger, and fear. I am grateful to Terry McDermott for contributing his poetry to this project to comfort women who experience post-abortion heartache.

WHITE RIBBON DAY

An aborted child still has a mother,
Jesus loves her like no other.
You likely feel sincere regret,
But know that Jesus has paid your debt.
Envision being at the foot of the cross.
Hand to Jesus all of your loss.
Be honest and share your heart,
Every day impossible to start.
Though your child has moved on,
There really will be a new dawn.
There is a time for everything.
The day will come to be with your King.
Your child is already there.
The Lord taking very good care.
You will hold your child once again,
Now is the time for your heart to mend.
You're forgiven because of His grace,
Thank the Lord and seek His face.
Speak to Him like your best friend,
He truly is the Beginning and the End.

He will protect you from all the lies,
Let the tears flow as your heart cries.
Focus on white ribbon day,
When you and your child will forever play.

A PRAYER FOR ALL MOTHERS

I pray for mothers whose kids drive them wild
For every mother of a preborn child.
I pray for mothers who cannot be,
For them to cling to Jesus, His Blood, and the tree.
I pray for mothers who gave their child away,
For their suffering day after day.
For a mother of a child never born,
And for her heart trampled and torn.
I pray for her regrets and fears,
I especially pray for her tears.
May every child look their mother in the eye,
My ultimate prayer, they won't have to die.

GRACE ALONE

As Jesus holds me near,
I wonder why I am here.
The result of a wrong choice,
Before a song came from my voice.
I never left the starting gate,
Never allowed to carry the weight.
During the dark night of your soul,
I wonder if you regret your role?
Though critically wounded is your heart,
It is never too late to make a new start.
I pray for the mom I never knew,
Handing her needs to Faithful and True.
Jesus, bring her to her knees,
Till Your love is all she sees.
A woman broken in two,
Does not have to be forever blue
I forgive my mom as I hand her to You,
Love her Jesus, like she never knew.

LONELY ARMS

Oh, what a mother goes through,
When she gives up baby blue.
Days when I couldn't get out of bed,
Days full of nothing but dread.
A broken heart seemingly beyond repair,
Looking out the window with a hollow stare.
Thinking about when I was a little girl,
Dancing with dad, giving me a twirl.
Why did everything turn out so wrong,
Oh, to start over how I long.
How can it be,
I've lost part of me.
Can I ever turn the page,
Move beyond this painful stage?
My heart broken in two,
A deep shade of dark blue.
God, I pray if You are real,
It is the time for You to reveal.
The emptiness seems beyond repair,
Days like this, I just don't care.

Is there grace enough these days,
Is it time to be the one who prays?
Help me place my trust in You,
By default, nothing else I can do.
Is that a smile I see on Your face,
Your love for me beyond time and space?
I chose life for baby blue,
A mother's love through and through.
I trust in eternity,
Where I eventually long to be.
You are the God of heaven and the second chance,
Where my child and I will forever dance.
Simply wait for what's in store,
Your lonely arms you'll have no more.

A DAD AND HIS DAUGHTER

What does it take to be a man,
Embrace your child, take her hand.
See past today and lift up a prayer,
God will help you if you dare.
Ask for wisdom to not believe the lies,
With abortion more than one heart dies.
For your child you need to choose life,
You will avoid years of strife.
Early on her little heart will beat,
An awesome, incredible feat.
Before long she'll kick soccer balls,
Maybe skin a knee when she falls.
When this young woman you give away,
You will never, ever forget that day.
In your heart she'll always be the best,
Better than all the rest.
She will be the clay and you her earthly potter,
Eternally special, a dad and his daughter.

LONELY TEARDROPS

A lonely woman asked for prayer,
My question prompted a stare.
"If Jesus stood here out of the blue,
What would you like Him to do?"
She replied with a simple plea,
She softly whispered, "Hug me."
Abortion, her recent story,
She needed Jesus in His glory.
I was broken in two,
My heart pierced through.
Hard not to cry,
Looking for wings to fly.
Words that brought me to my knees,
Praying for a holy breeze.
A cloud of sadness over her head,
A lonely woman trying not to wake up dead.
I prayed the best I could,
At the foot of the cross is where I stood.
I walked away with the sky crying,
Thought of Jesus and His dying.

Were His teardrops on my face,
Beyond grateful to have been in that place.
Blessed to have the woman's back,
Though the words I surely lacked.
Placed her needs at the throne of grace,
The ultimate celestial place.
Trusting Jesus was in that space,
A baby teardrop on her face.

THE DAY BEFORE TOMORROW

Yesterday used to be tomorrow,
Void of all sorrow.
If the present were yesterday,
My little girl, an execution stay.
Then I could forever dance,
Having been given a second chance.
Yet going back cannot be,
Forever it becomes history.
I wasn't blind, but I could not see,
Today a rendezvous with reality.
Gone before she could appear,
In a forest, like a deer.
Her life a book with only a cover,
Never even knew her mother.
"In the beginning . . . the end,"
Her torn heart, never to mend.
My broken heart I must confess,
Thankful Jesus will not love me less.

FOREVER WINTER

I feel so very cold,
If only I'd been told.
If someone had come alongside,
The two of us would not have died.
You were never allowed to run your race,
My heart's dead, taking up space.
Way too young for the responsibility,
Outside pressure overwhelming me.
My loneliness cuts to the bone,
My only prayer simply a groan.
If only truth had carried the day,
I believed the lies, now I pay.
Now I see, when once I was blind,
Just needed someone to be kind.
Never close to feeling so alone,
I live with a heart of stone.
God alone knows my fate,
So for now I simply wait.
Is there grace enough this day,
To turn my December into May?

STORM THE HEAVENS

Know what you gotta know,
Do what you gotta do.
Go where you gotta go,
And always pray for baby blue.
Even if no execution stay,
Pray it anyway.
Pray together, pray alone,
Pray like you've been chilled to the bone.
Prayers that cut like a knife,
See her tears, end the strife.
Prayers which are not mild,
Pray with the faith of a child.
Call upon the Name of the Lord,
Every prayer in heaven stored.
Seek His face, He will be found,
Let Your heart become unwound.
Your eyes and His will meet,
The silent sound of sandaled feet.

BEYOND BABY BLUE

"Mother, look at my sonogram,
It clearly proves, I am.
You will see my heart beat,
Our eyes might even meet.
This is not what you planned,
But ending my life must be banned."
At an abortion clinic two people enter,
A door closes at the center.
One forever damaged; one forever dead,
A life of love choose instead.
An overwhelming challenge you now face,
There is an option in your case.
Adoption is an act of love,
Like letting go of a newborn dove.
The gift of life you will set free,
And in time you will let it be.
Pray for courage to make the right choice,
Listen for a gentle voice.
Love beyond all measure,
As you release your little treasure.

WHEN JESUS WALKED

At the soft sound of Jesus' feet,
The dragon ends in defeat.
Jehovah knew from the time of Eve,
That Mary would conceive.
His alabaster jar placed in a manger,
God invaded earth as a stranger.
Mercy and grace override a travesty,
The One and Only, Majesty.
The eyes of Faithful and True,
Broken and blue.
He walked and He bled,
A relentless sea of Red.
The scourging at the pillar,
For most men, it was a killer.
And He walked,
Rarely talked.
Oh, how my heart mourns,
Blood flows from the crown of thorns.
He walked on,
Bringing us a new dawn.

Via Dolorosa, the Way of Sorrow,
So there would be a new tomorrow.
A river of red,
Way before our God was dead.
My sins in the form of a nail,
On the cross, Jesus, I did impale.
My hand and His forever locked,
I long to witness, when Jesus walked.

MY HEART'S CRY

Been to hell and back,
Feel like the deck is stacked.
Unanswered questions trouble me,
I struggle to let it be.
Yet my faith refuses to quit,
A little light in my heart is still lit.
Beyond the God of a second chance,
The God of no chance takes a stance.
This may not be my original plan,
I long to play my part in the family of man.
Sometimes doubt continues to rage,
But I believe God will turn the page.
A gift beyond measure,
A child I will treasure.
Holy Spirit protect me from the lie,
I will give this child wings to fly.
The day will come, the child will stand,
Grateful to be able to take her hand.

A MOTHER'S LAMENT

A race never run,
A song never sung.
A first step never taken,
A precious life forsaken.
First words never spoken,
A tiny body torn and broken.
Denied the privilege of prayer,
The ultimate gift so rare.
Eyes that never see,
Jesus, His Blood, and the tree.
Regrettable seeds were sown,
If only I had known.
Is there grace enough this day,
For an eternal execution stay?
A mother full of fears,
Only You can take away her tears
Yet my heart knows Jesus is the Way,
By faith I'll be with Him forever and a day.

SILENT SUFFERING

Suffering in silence,
Because of the violence.
I walked through a door,
My child to be never more.
When I walked out she was dead,
I am still going out of my head.
Needed to hear that Jesus will forgive,
My only chance to once again live.
Now I take my loss,
I have laid it at the cross.
Handed Jesus all my shame,
Moved beyond all the blame.
To the cross my guilt I pin,
Now the healing will finally begin.
Hearing the soft sound of His feet,
As Jesus' eyes and mine are about to meet.

HANDLE WITH PRAYER

When I'm down and out,
Feeling like I've lost the bout,
My heart broken in two,
Sometimes a prayer will do.
When the call on my life,
Provides overwhelming strife,
As deeds of darkness make me blue,
I do believe a prayer will do.
When I feel all alone,
Chilled right to the bone,
Doubting what I know to be true,
I'm beyond grateful that a prayer will do.
When the dark night of my soul,
Seems to take an eternal toll,
As the walls collapse and I haven't a clue,
I look up, trusting a prayer will do.
When the air I breathe is soaked in tears,
And I'm surrounded by all my fears,
When I feel over and through,
I truly know a prayer will do.

WHAT HAPPENED TO YOUR BLOOD?

Your body rose from the dead,
But what happened to the sea of red?
Father, why do I ponder?
Spirit, why do I wonder?
Jesus, do these thoughts really matter?
All I see is Your Blood and its splatter.
What happened to Your Blood in the Garden,
That played such a role in Your celestial pardon?
Where is the Blood that ran down Your face,
From the crown of thorns and Your perceived disgrace?
I hear the whip crack,
Where is the Blood that poured from Your back?
As the fists beat Your face,
Your Blood all over the place.
I see You nailed to the cross,
Where is all the Blood that You lost?
Your Blood dripped from the tree,
Why can I not let it be?
As I seek the very most of You,
Wondering where is Your Blood, makes me blue.

Jesus, You are no longer here,
But I wonder if Your Blood is near?
In a way my mind cannot understand,
could Your Blood still be in that foreign land?
Or is Your Blood, that allows me to pray,
close to my heart, showing me the Way?
I wait on You, because I need to know,
What happened to Your Blood, that I love so?

THE STORYTELLER

Three months living outside the womb,
My first birthday celebrated in my room
My young mother made the right choice,
She heard my tiny voice.
Avoiding years of untold strife,
Taking my hand, not my life.
She walked a mile in my shoes,
Realized there was much to lose.
Satan's tears a gift of joy,
As mom saved her little boy.

RUNAWAY

My walk seems to be a run,
Always feeling over and done.
I run ahead of You,
Faithful and True.
I run when I should walk,
Hurtful words when I shouldn't talk.
I run away,
When I should stay.
I run for cover,
Not to my Eternal Lover.
Running on empty I seem to do,
When I should, run to You.

TEARS

Nothing else to do,
Nowhere else to go.
Jesus, I turn to You,
Though much I'll never know.
Brokenness I long for,
Take me to the floor.
Like Mary, I sit at Your feet,
Waiting for our eyes to meet.
I pray for mothers whose choice they'd erase,
Wondering whose tears are on my face?

A WHITE BOY'S BLUES

Why does a white boy love the blues,
Feel like I've nothing left to lose?
At home in Mississippi with the Blacks,
On my face, tears and their tracks.
Love Jesus with most of my heart,
Gave me a brand new start.
Yet I wonder, ponder, and doubt,
A thread of melancholy weaved throughout.
Most things I just can't let be,
When it impacts, Jesus, His Blood and the tree.
I have a passion for causes and don't know why,
Probably will till the day I die.
Some days my heart will soar,
Believing there is so much more.
Yet it's easily broken in two,
Pierced through and through.
Wonder if God made a mistake,
Placing me in this state?
A witness on the wall,
Waiting to answer the call.

Long for heaven with a sigh,
But I don't want to die.
Long ago I quit asking why,
Ignore me when I lie.
A white-hot spirit of discontent,
Helps my soul pay the rent.
Feel the need to fight the giant,
So hard to be compliant.
Hate the ultimate child abuse,
Sixty million dead, necks in a noose.
Good and evil reside in me,
I wonder how can it be?
Spiritual battles wear me out,
Lead to a dark night of doubt.
Sometimes I feel so alone,
When all I need is the Cornerstone.

MARTIN LUTHER KING HALL

Graduated from UC Davis Law in 1972,
I still believe in Faithful and True.
Can almost see a tear in His eye,
Long ago I quit asking why.
See the dissension at UCD,
And I wonder, how can it be?
We all bleed crimson red,
Why the evil and waking up dead?
So many have bought the lie,
Their mantra is others must die.
They truly do have much to lose,
Forever and a day I'll sing the blues.
Spent many a day in MLK Hall,
Still need his voice to stand tall.

"The Lord is close to the brokenhearted and saves those who are crushed in spirit."

Ps 34:18 NIV

Conclusion

Jeanne DeFazio

Nelson Mandela's poem "Letting Go" inspired me to publish this book.

> "Letting Go" is a poignant and powerful reminder of the importance of forgiveness and release. Nelson Mandela's words offer a message of hope and unity, encouraging us to let go of grudges and bitterness and embrace the humanity in others. Through its moving verse, the poem inspires us to find peace and happiness by recognizing that holding onto the past only hinders our ability to move forward. A truly inspiring work, "Letting Go" serves as a timeless call to action for all of us to strive for unity and understanding.[1]

Brother Curtis Almquist, SSJE, explains:

> Normal will never return, I hope not." An African-American friend said this to me recently. She was speaking about the experience of injustice and suffering that has been so poignantly exposed during the coronavirus pandemic: the strains and inequities in healthcare, the economic disparity, the hijacking of hope and trust, the infectious cynicism, the splay of racism. We have right now both the need and the opportunity to make meaningful changes in how we live and share life together. How to begin?[2]

---

1. See Moleveld, "Powerful Poem by Nelson Mandela," para. 17.
2. Almquist, "Making Meaning," 10.

About the Authors

JULIA C. DAVIS EARNED an EdM from the Harvard Graduate School of Education, and an EdM from Bouvé College of Health Sciences at Northeastern University. She has held teaching certificates in New York, Massachusetts, and the District of Columbia and has been certified as an assistant principal and as an assistant special education supervisor. Julia has taught in the public and private sector in community-based programs including METCO, summer STEP opportunities for underrepresented populations in science and technology, and Head Start. She has served as a member of Parent's Advocacy Group for Massachusetts supporting FAPE and mainstreaming special education students. She has taught pre-K through all twelve grades, adult non-readers, limited English language learners, and GED preparation courses. Julia taught internationally as an undergraduate exchange student in a special education program based in Newnham on Severn, Gloucester Shire, England, which operated under the auspices of Antioch College in Ohio. Julia and her husband Dan have three children and three grandchildren. They attend the International Family Church in North Reading, Massachusetts.

JEANNE DEFAZIO is a former SAG/AFTRA (Screen Actors Guild—American Federation of Television and Radio Artists) actress of Spanish Italian descent, who played supporting parts in theater, movies, and television series, then served the marginalized in the drama of real life. She became a teacher of second-language-learner children in the barrios of San Diego. She completed a BA in history at the University of California, Davis, MAR in theology at Gordon-Conwell Theological Seminary, and a Cal State Teach English Language Learners program. From 2009 to the present, she has served as an Athanasian teaching scholar at Gordon-Conwell's multicultural Boston Center for urban ministerial education.

TERRY MCDERMOTT holds a BA from Santa Clara University; a JD from the University of California, Davis, School of Law; and an LL.M from the University of California, Berkeley, School of Law. He is a lecturer in law, emeritus, Sacramento State University.

Bibliography

Almquist, Curtis. "Making Meaning." *Cowley Magazine*, Fall 2020. https://issuu.com/ssje/docs/2020_cowley_fall___pages.

Kortsmit, Katherine, et al. "Abortion Surveillance—United States, 2021." *Morbidity and Mortality Weekly Report Surveillance Summaries* 72 (2023) 1–29. https://www.cdc.gov/mmwr/volumes/72/ss/ss7209a1.htm?s_cid=ss7209a1_w.

Mathis, Wilma Faye. *Jesus among the Homeless: Successful Strategies of Christian Ministers to the Marginalized.* Eugene, OR: Wipf & Stock, 2023.

Moleveld, Vincent. "A Powerful Poem by Nelson Mandela about Letting Go." *Online Gallery*, December 5, 2018. https://onlinegallery.art/en/blog/a-powerful-poem-by-nelson-mandela-about-letting-go-243/.

Soon, Brian. "How Music Have Changed My Life." *True Story* (blog), n.d. https://notionpress.com/en/story/read/401/how-music-have-changed-my-life.

Welsh NHS Confederation. "Arts, Health and Well-Being." https://www.nhsconfed.org/system/files/media/Arts-health-and-wellbeing_0.pdf.

www.ingramcontent.com/pod-product-compliance
Lightning Source LLC
Chambersburg PA
CBHW061301040426
42444CB00010B/2471